Words of Praise for
Living in the Yellow

"*Living in The Yellow* has inspired me to know that God has a plan for us in the pauses and waiting stages of life. The daily titles and Bible verses stick and resonate with me; the challenges and journal prompts move me to make a positive change in my attitude while living in the yellow stages of my life. The prayers that are written each day connect me with God and inspire me to trust that He is working in my life."

— Millen Gelilang Argueta
Medical Missionary & Health Clinic Volunteer

"This 21-day devotional is well written and practical. It will be a positive way to start the day. Readers will appreciate the daily prayer and daily action item. I also love that it includes space for journaling."

— Zalika Bishop
Adventist Young Professionals Chapter Coordinator & Church Ministry Leader

"Whether young or old, this very understandable book will help people stay hopeful, positive, and joyful as they face many life challenges. This 21-day devotional will guide people to God with the Bible verses included, the prayers that they can pray, and the challenges that they can do daily. It can help readers step up for great opportunities and extraordinary growth."

— Ryan Mamora
Northern New England Conference Pastor & Adventist Indonesian Youth and Young Adult Ministry Convention Spiritual Leader

Living in the Yellow

What Are You Waiting For?

A 21-Day Devotional & Journal

Marselinny Mawuntu

TEACH Services, Inc.
P U B L I S H I N G
www.TEACHServices.com • (800) 367-1844

World rights reserved. This book or any portion thereof may not be copied or reproduced in any form or manner whatever, except as provided by law, without the written permission of the publisher, except by a reviewer who may quote brief passages in a review.

The author assumes full responsibility for the accuracy of all facts and quotations as cited in this book. The opinions expressed in this book are the author's personal views and interpretations, and do not necessarily reflect those of the publisher.

This book is provided with the understanding that the publisher is not engaged in giving spiritual, legal, medical, or other professional advice. If authoritative advice is needed, the reader should seek the counsel of a competent professional.

Copyright © 2024 Marselinny Mawuntu
Copyright © 2024 TEACH Services, Inc.
ISBN-13: 978-1-4796-1778-4 (Paperback)
ISBN-13: 978-1-4796-1779-1 (ePub)
Library of Congress Control Number: 2024910531

All Scripture quotations, unless otherwise indicated, are taken from the New International Version. Copyright © 1973, 1978, 1984, 2011 by Biblica, Inc®. Used by permission. All rights reserved worldwide.

All Scripture quotations marked NKJV are taken from the New King James Version®. Copyright © 1990 by Thomas Nelson. Used by permission. All rights reserved.

Scripture quotations marked NLT are taken from the New Living Translation. Copyright © 1996, 2004, 2015 by Tyndale House Foundation. Used by permission of Tyndale House Publishers, Inc., Carol Stream, Illinois 60188. All rights reserved.

Interior photographs by the author.

Published by

*Dedicated to my parents, family, mentors, supporters,
and friends (you know who you are)—
Thank you for being there through every season.*

*And, of course, I can't forget, our heavenly Father.
This book would not have been possible without Him.
To God be the glory! Thank You, Jesus.*

Table of Contents

Preface ix

Day 1: New Year … New Me? 13
(Isa. 43:18–19, NIV)

Day 2: Resilience 16
(Job 23:10, NKJV)

Day 3: Living in the Yellow. 19
(Ps. 27:13–14, NKJV)

Day 4: Peace Above Any Storm 22
(Matt. 8:26–27, NIV)

Day 5: Forty-One Is on the Way 25
(2 Cor. 5:7, NKJV)

Day 6: The Other Side 28
(1 Cor. 2:9, NIV)

Day 7: Twenty-Twenty Vision in a Blur 31
(John 13:7, NLT)

Day 8: Don't Forget to Smile! 34
(Prov. 17:22, NIV)

Day 9: Broken into Beautiful 37
(Eph. 2:10, NLT)

Day 10: RESTART 40
(Heb. 12:1, NKJV)

Day 11: Chosen to Shine. 43
(Matt. 5:16, NKJV)

Day 12: A Winning Attitude 46
(1 Peter 3:15, NKJV)

Day 13: Blessings in Disguise 49
        (Eccles. 3:1, NKJV)

Day 14: Finding Joy in the Desert 52
        (Acts 8:26, NKJV)

Day 15: No One Is an Island. 55
        (Prov. 17:17, NIV)

Day 16: Stuck in the Muck. 58
        (Ps. 40:1–2, NIV)

Day 17: Thank You, COVID-19. 61
        (Neh. 8:10, NKJV)

Day 18: Beginning or Ending 64
        (Matt. 9:17, NIV)

Day 19: Qualifying the Called. 67
        (Exod. 4:2–3, NLT)

Day 20: Worry Is a Waste 70
        (Matt. 6:27, NIV)

Day 21: What Are You Waiting For? 73
        (Jer. 29:11, NIV)

Afterword. 76

Preface

Sometimes we miss out
On the things along the way
To where we're going ...

As the sun rises, a new day begins. Every day, we are faced with many uncertainties and unforeseen unknowns that seem unfathomable. For me, I remember a particular incident when I was little, and waiting for an outcome was like whispering in a crowd, but it is in these moments where you discover the "thing" you have been waiting for is just around the corner—wait for it.

"I was six feet under for about six seconds before I realized what was happening. Seconds seemed like eternity to me, and there were only two options. *Sink or swim*, I thought to myself, but I was stuck in the middle. I did not want to sink, but I also did not know how to swim. Like a traffic light, there is red, yellow, or green; I was in the yellow ..." (to be continued).

As we journey together for these next twenty-one days, they say it takes about three weeks to form or start a habit (research recommended) and about three months to maintain a lifestyle (ninety days). Although sources may differ, this 21/90 "rule" of building a habit and keeping that lifestyle can help inspire one to know that change is possible over time. However, it is consistency that is key.

No matter what you are currently waiting for, whether it is a job, spouse, or career, the list could go on forever. Quite honestly, often we get so fixated on the "what's next" that we fail to realize the blessings right in front of us. Yes, we may be waiting for that promotion or raise at work, but we groan and grumble about doing the extra work to get there. Everything may seem tedious or mundane since we are not in the present. Instead of the here and now, what does the future hold?

Times of waiting remind me of my experiences working in the hospital emergency room (ER), intensive care unit (ICU), and even outpatient care centers. Hours upon hours of waiting, you come in as a patient for a medical problem and sit in the "waiting room" for what seems like an eternity. Other patients come and go, and you can't help but start to be a little bit impatient. Waiting for results, a diagnosis, any answers to your questions of why you feel the way you feel leaves you numb, and you just close your eyes.... Until, when you least expect it, the door opens.

I don't know about you, but even though I don't know what the future holds, I know who holds the future, and it is safe with Him. During the coronavirus (COVID-19) pandemic, I started to blog and journal my highs and lows amidst an unprecedented time of chaos and uncertainty. Through it all, I realized that when we praise God for the blessings instead of pondering over the burdens, everything becomes beautiful. So, friend, during these next twenty-one days, always remember:

"Just hold on—it gets better."

*If only we could
Go back in time and see that
Everything worked out.*

Day 1

New Year ... New Me?

"Forget the former things; do not dwell on the past. See, I am doing a new thing! Now it springs up; do you not perceive it? I am making a way in the wilderness and streams in the wasteland."

(Isa. 43:18–19, NIV)

New Year's Resolution #1: Grow closer daily to God. #2: Eat better. #3: Exercise more. And the list goes on and on. Sound familiar? If it does, you're not alone. I'll have to admit, this is actually me every year. This year is no different, but does a new year really mean ... a new me?

As we go on to the following weeks of a new year, everything feels pretty much the same. There was no *poof* or sudden change as the clock struck midnight that we are completely changed into a new person. Change is a process; change takes time. The only way we are transformed into the image of God is to behold Him daily. By beholding, we become changed, but most times, we have no idea what to do next. We are left in the desert during our dry seasons, and we don't know where to go. We don't have the slightest direction, but it is in these seasons that God is using our struggle to prepare us for the victory. Our next season may seem like a blur right now, but pray and don't give up hope! Cling onto His promises that He will never leave us nor forsake us. Our heavenly Father loves us too much to leave us how we are in this trying season. He is preparing us to embrace the new and trust that He has something better in store.

However, we don't have to wait for a new year to change. His mercies are new every morning. Another day is a new opportunity to wait for God to reveal His plans for our lives. We shouldn't need to sit around and do nothing in the waiting but wait actively. Sounds kind of contradictory, but God doesn't simply want us to wait while doing absolutely nothing.

When we don't know the next step, we must pray to do the next right thing. Pray for His divine direction. He will never let us down!

Life is a car ride
You may face bumps in the road,
But you keep driving.

Prayer

Dear Lord, thank You for new beginnings. Every day is a new day to grow and know more about You. I pray this journey is a start to the lasting change and transformation that only You can do. In Jesus' name, amen.

Challenge

While you are waiting for something, what is something new that you always wanted to learn to do? Pray about it and take action as the Lord wills. You never know what good is in store next!

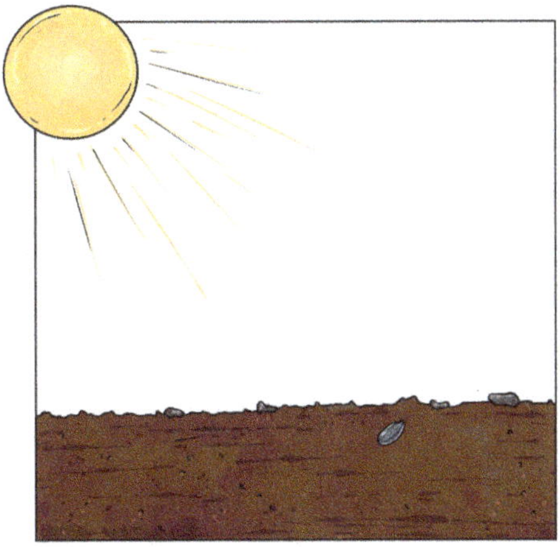

| Day 2

Resilience

*"But He knows the way that I take;
when He has tested me, I shall come forth as gold."*

(Job 23:10, NKJV)

That was my theme word one year: Resilience. The Oxford dictionary defines this word as "the capacity to recover quickly from difficulties; toughness."[1] Its second definition says, "the ability of a substance or object to spring back into shape; elasticity."[2] Wow. I chose this word for many different reasons. After finishing a forty-day Bible devotional plan called "Growing in Resilience: A Prayer Journey," it kind of changed my whole perspective on what it truly means to be resilient. The Marselinny dictionary would define this term as "no matter what happens in life, just keep moving forward … in becoming a better person than you were yesterday." What's your definition?

When I read and reflect on the story of Job, it's heavy! There is a lot to swallow—let alone digest—but this whole book in the Bible reveals such a greater picture of trusting and having faith in God, even in the most trying times of your life. God is STILL GOOD, even when our circumstances are not, and He is and will be with us every step of the way. Just like pure gold is refined in the fire, there will be times where things get a little heated in our lives. Things don't go as planned. We may lose our jobs. We may encounter financial crises. We may endure a divorce that we never saw coming. We may lose e-v-e-r-y-t-h-i-n-g (I'm sure Job didn't see any of those tragedies

---

[1] Bryan Robinson, "Why The Word For 2021 Is 'Resilience' And How It Affects Mental Health," Forbes, https://1ref.us/mm1.
[2] Ibid.

coming), but whatever the case may be, just like God was with Job during the hardest, darkest times of his life, the Lord will be with us. We need to pray for a faith greater than fear.

Just like the definitions stated, resilience is the ability to recover quickly … toughness … being able to spring back from things that may misshape us … elasticity. By God's grace, there is a comeback from our setback. We just have to step back and let the Lord show us He has our back. For me, resilience is not simply being able to handle the obstacles and take the lemons that life gives us, but trusting in the Lord that we can bounce back with joy instead of regret. Only then can we truly become pure gold: another definition of resilience.

Give when not able
Though you can't see a return,
Trust the Rewarder.

Prayer

Dear heavenly Father, you made us resilient. Help us when we don't feel like we are. Teach us how we can be more like You, in Your image and Your likeness. In Jesus' name, amen.

Challenge

Prayerfully decide on a theme word for your current year right now and claim it in the name of Jesus! May that word (noun/verb/adjective/adverb) be a constant reminder for your sure growth this year.

18 *Living in the Yellow*

Day 3

Living in the Yellow

"I would have lost heart, unless I had believed that I would see the goodness of the LORD in the land of the living. Wait on the LORD; be of good courage, and He shall strengthen your heart; wait, I say, on the LORD!"

(Ps. 27:13–14, NKJV)

When you think of the color yellow, what comes to mind? Maybe the sun, smiley emojis, flowers, just to name a few. Often, this color is associated with brightness, happiness, and friendliness in life. However, sometimes, it can also bring about a sense of uncertainty. A caution sign, construction work, and most notably, the yellow traffic light. It actually could be a pretty stressful color—stuck in the middle between red or green—not knowing whether to take a risk or just play it safe. Now, don't get me wrong; I'm not suggesting you run a yellow light every time, but there are times where we are easily about to pass the traffic light and it turns yellow. It would be dangerous just to slow and stop in the middle of the road. So we keep going to avoid putting ourselves in harm's way. Ultimately, it really depends on timing and where we are in that current situation.

Similarly, in life, we contemplate, *Should I stop? Should I go? Should I wait?* I'm sure we've all been there at some point before, but is it a crazy thought to think that, right now, we are all living in the yellow? Whether it's work, school, career, relationship, or that bank account to miraculously be filled, we are all waiting for something. We are all "in the waiting," expecting something in our lives to change for the better, but what if our seasons of waiting are where we can find joy and peace? Faith in Christ grows as we truly seek His plan and purpose for our lives, not ours.

If you know me, I love sunflowers. A few years ago, I was able to check "Visit a Sunflower Maze" off my bucket list. It was an a-maze-ing sight to see so many beautiful, strong flowers amidst the downpour of rain later that day. My favorite part of these yellow creations? They turn to face the sun as they grow. Likewise, in our times of waiting, may we experience growth while looking to the Sun of righteousness as our main source of light and love as we live this life. I don't know exactly what you are waiting for, but what I do know is that God is with you every single moment of your waiting season. Yes, it can be hard. Yes, it can also be rewarding. As our patience grows, I pray and believe the greatest hope we have in faith and acceptance is awaiting Jesus' second coming for His return to take us home. Until then, keep fighting the good fight; don't lose hope! Be of good courage. Thrive while living in the yellow.... Wait, I say, on the Lord!

You don't always get
What you want in this short life
And that is okay.

Prayer

Dear God, You know the end from the beginning. You know when we rise and when we fall. Help us in our times of fear and doubt, and may we always look to You in every single situation. In Jesus' name, amen.

Challenge

While you wait, it's hard to push through the obstacles that stand in your way but try anyway. What is one thing that you can positively change your perspective and mindset on? Write it down!

Day 3   21

| Day 4

Peace Above Any Storm

*"He replied, 'You of little faith, why are you so afraid?' Then he got up
and rebuked the winds and the waves, and it was completely calm.
The men were amazed and asked, 'What kind of man is this?
Even the winds and the waves obey him!'"*

(Matt. 8:26–27, NIV)

Let's cut to the chase. We know everyone was talking about it. And I don't mean hand sanitizer, toilet paper, or water bottles, I mean the coronavirus aka COVID-19 (but those things are important too!). Life was on a pause. Stores were closed, schools were closed, and social areas were closed, but why don't we daily open up our minds to the good in life that still exists? Even though it seemed like everything was canceled, faith will never be canceled. Hope will never be canceled. Most of all, love will never be canceled.

What does it mean to have "peace above the storm"? One of my favorite stories from the Bible talks about this so clearly. Read with me from verses 23–27 of Matthew chapter 8: "Then he got into the boat and his disciples followed him." Now, this first verse I tend to overlook because I've read this story so many times over, but the key part that was newly revealed to me was that Jesus gets into the boat first. We follow. Not the other way around. If we let Him lead, even though we face some pretty scary times, trust and know that we're going to be okay because He goes before us.

Next, verse 24, "Suddenly a furious storm came up on the lake, so that the waves swept over the boat. But Jesus was sleeping." Powerful thing to take note of: suddenly. When I think of that word, I imagine that, you know, things are going just fine, and then out of nowhere, something unexpected happens—something you didn't foresee or couldn't plan for. However, what does the last part of that verse say? Jesus was sleeping. Let me ask you this: When you're sleeping, are you worried about the things happening around you? No. Now, fast-forward to the last two verses in 26 and 27; the highlight I would say is that Jesus has the power to change things around, a complete 180, peace above the storm. Will you let Him in your boat?

Amidst the variability of our current situations, we can be certain of one thing: God is still in control. Not letting your fear get the best of you is easier said than done, but I know that if we fix our eyes on Him instead of the storm, we will be just fine. Remember that even while a virus spreads, we can still spread peace to those around us (at least six feet away, of course)!

God's timing is best;
Even when you want to rush
The process—trust it.

Prayer

Dear Lord, we know it's hard to thank You for the storms, but without them, we would never experience the peace of when You calm them. So thank You for the storm. Help us to trust more. In Jesus' name, amen.

Challenge

What can you do to bless someone else in his or her own life storm, while you are battling yours? It may not be easy, but you have the Commander of all storms on your side.

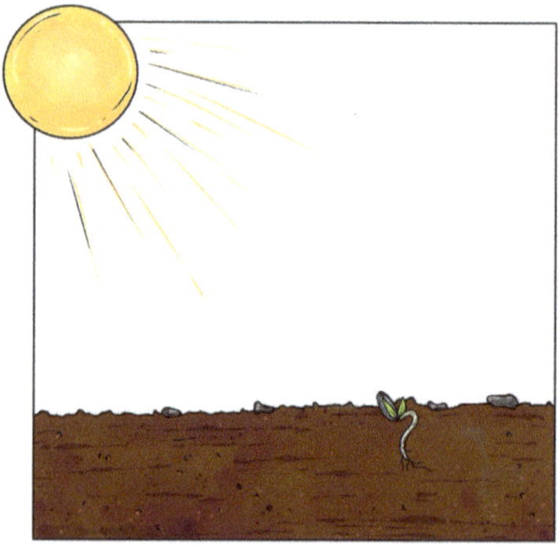

| Day 5

Forty-One Is on the Way

"For we walk by faith, not by sight"

(2 Cor. 5:7, NKJV)

Day 1. Day 2. Day 3. Quarantine. And days drag on. Similarly in the Bible, the Israelites wandered through the wilderness for forty years. Can you believe it? But year forty-one came and a next generation entered the Promised Land. It rained for forty days and forty nights, but day forty-one came and the rain ended. Just like that! Can you believe it? Though quarantines are over, let us remember:

1. There is HOPE in the HOLE. When you picture a deep hole in the ground, you often can't see the bottom ... and if you happen to fall in, everywhere you turn is just filled with emptiness. You look around—nothing. But what happens when you look up? Hope. There's a light above that reminds you it's going to be okay. Don't forget: if there's a way in, there's *always* a way out.
2. There is PURPOSE in the PIT. Just like the story of Joseph, one of my favorites in the Bible, his so-called brothers threw him into an empty pit, left for dead, and later sold him as a slave. The story doesn't end there though. Hallelujah! From the pit to the palace, Joseph had a purpose from God to save His people from famine and hard times in the years to come. Moral: never give up on your calling.
3. There is DIRECTION in the DARK. When we can't see what's ahead, we're reminded in Psalm chapter 119 that His word is lamp unto our feet and a light unto our path (v. 105). Truly, life has its times of pure darkness and hopelessness. In these times when we don't know where

to go or what to do, remember that if we didn't have the dark below, we'd never see the stars above.

During an unprecedented season, I was able to go for a walk with my sister, my brother-in-law, and my face mask. Of course, all the parks were closed, but we happened to find a secluded area with beautiful blossoms and what seemingly looked like a river. I say seemingly because it really wasn't flowing. It was stagnant and very thin. *That's such a sad river*, I thought. However, what I didn't realize was that on the other side of the bridge was the most beautiful, wide, flowing river with a fountain in the middle surrounded by ducks and flower petals. Then it clicked. Wow. In one way or another, we are on one side of the bridge, but when the time comes, we will get to the other side. "This too shall pass." Forty-one is on the way. ... Will you believe it?

*It's okay to spend
Time with yourself and the One
Who gives time to you.*

Prayer

Dear Lord, the unknown is always uncertain and may feel scary sometimes to imagine what lies ahead. You are already there, so remind us of Your way. It's the best. In Jesus' name, amen.

Challenge

Although we do not know what the future holds, we ultimately know He holds our future, and that is Jesus Christ. How can you share this truth with a neighbor who may not know Him?

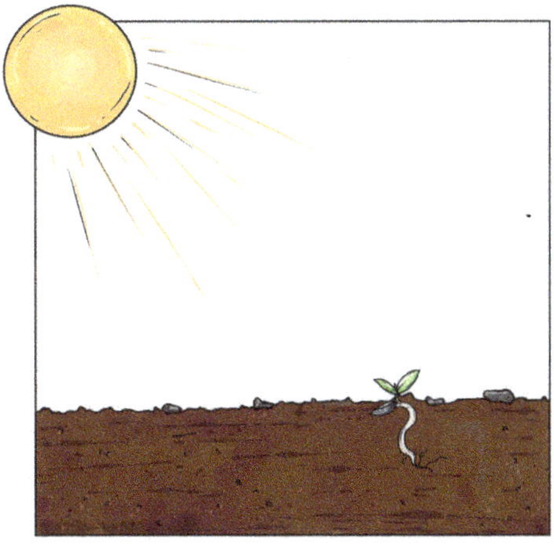

| Day 6

The Other Side

"However, as it is written: 'What no eye has seen, what no ear has heard, and what no human mind has conceived'—the things God has prepared for those who love him."

(1 Cor. 2:9, NIV)

Ever since the COVID-19 lockdown, it was hard to see the silver lining, but we slowly, but surely, reached the other side. To reflect on past experiences, I wanted to share a snippet of my old school newspaper article that was published years ago, and I pray that it sheds some light on the tremendous impact that the journey makes on the destination:

The best view comes after the hardest climb—it doesn't get any realer than that. This semester, I had the chance to take a rock climbing class. Before the first day of class, I was second-guessing myself and my willingness to take the class. One, I'm afraid of heights, and two, I'm afraid of heights. Looking down at the ground below me as I inch my way up a mountain wasn't exactly on my list of happy places. With uncertainty and anxiety, I made the decision to finally get over my fear. … As I made my way up, I thought, "This isn't hard. I got this." When I passed the halfway point, I stopped. I found no footholds or handholds, and I was near giving up. I wanted to get to the top and be done with it. My arms were aching; my legs numb from the cold. Then I remembered to pause and look around. Take deep breaths and take my time. If I hastened to the top, I might not see what would help me climb and miss the chances of finding a foundation for my feet to stand on and keep going. When I stopped rushing and looked up from a different angle, I saw a small crevice that I overlooked before. I put my right hand in it and hoisted myself up. I smeared a rock with my left foot and made it up to the top.... What I learned from the class is something I will keep with me forever: Sure, the top will be a great view, but how you get there is even greater.[3]

Although we may not know what the other side holds and may grapple with fear, anxiety, or doubt, rest assured that greater things are in store! God is able to do exceedingly abundantly above all that we ask or think, so why not allow Him to? Ultimately, when people ask me, "Where do you see yourself in one month, one year, ten years?" I'd say, "I don't know ... but I'll see you on the other side!" As we wait with anticipation what lies ahead toward the destination, may we never, ever forget the life-changing journey that led us there.

True friends never give
Up on you even when you
Give up on them, too.

Prayer

Dear mighty Savior, You are our rock in times of trouble. You are our anchor that holds us firm. Remind us to look up when we're feeling down, and help us to remember that heaven awaits us. In Jesus' name, amen.

Challenge

Go on a nature walk and find a smooth rock outside. On it, write down with a permanent marker one word that best describes who God is to you. Keep it as a token to remind you that the Rock of Ages is always with you and for you.

---

[3] Marsie Mawuntu, "It's the Climb," *Southern Accent*, April 7, 2016.

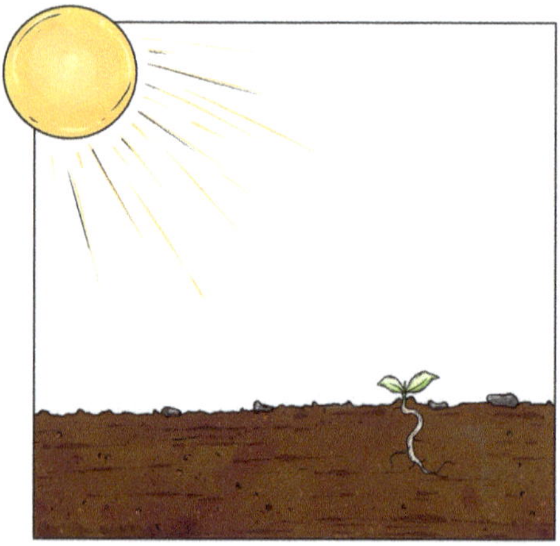

| Day 7

Twenty-Twenty Vision in a Blur

"Jesus replied, 'You don't understand now what I am doing, but someday you will.'"

(John 13:7, NLT)

Close your eyes and imagine that you have just journeyed through a thick, fierce forest, thinking you would never make it out. Now, you find yourself facing a bridge ... but no ordinary bridge. Its ancient wooden planks are broken; its edges are covered in fog. Would you take the first step? Many times in life, we are in a haze. We struggle with letting go of the past when we cannot see what is ahead. We grapple with taking risks when we cannot assume the outcome. This key Bible verse is centered on the story of Jesus and how He insists on washing Peter's feet. To Peter, the idea seems absolutely absurd, as he does not see the purpose. To Jesus, it had a greater meaning.

The year 2020 opened a new decade ... a new vision? Perfect 20/20 vision, right? Let's face it. Everything that year was pretty much an unsure blur, but when you think of it, in times of uncertainty, what clears up the fog? The wind. The Holy Spirit gives us clarity as we read the Bible and clearly see the truth of God's Word. When we see things through His lenses, everything makes sense and has purpose. Although we may not understand all that is happening now and complain about the negatives, just like a camera, if we shift our focus on the positives and reframe our thinking toward heavenly things, we find ourselves now looking beyond the tattered bridge and crisply seeing that what lies ahead is worth the struggle of today. Take the first step. It's an act of faith. It's up to us to continue the story until the last chapter. And trust me, with Jesus in the book—it ends well.

Here's a poem I wrote called "Her Story Is Not History" for a school's literary magazine:

"Fog clothes the forest; silence fills the air
But in the faint, far distance, there is a wood bridge
That stretches where no eye can see,
For miles and miles
And piles and piles of anxious weight
Wait at the start.
She is reluctant to take the first step
With gaps in the bridge
But eyes closed, she stumbles and finds herself
On the first tattered wooden plank.
To her,
The finish is unknown
And as the wind is tossed and blown,
Her story is not history;
No man can tell it otherwise.
Like a book that has no end
Until the end meets a beginning;
When an old chapter closes,
A new one begins."

Your story is not history either. Turn the page: Next chapter.

If you have a goal,
Go for it with all you have.
Tomorrow's not here.

Prayer

Dear Father God, we can't see the future or what's ahead of us. Only You know. Help us to trust in Your ways that are higher than ours, and direct our steps to Your purpose and plan for our lives. In Jesus' name, amen.

Challenge

Even if poetry is not your forte, grab a pen and paper and write out any of your thoughts to create some kind of free verse poem (doesn't need to rhyme) about what's going through your mind.

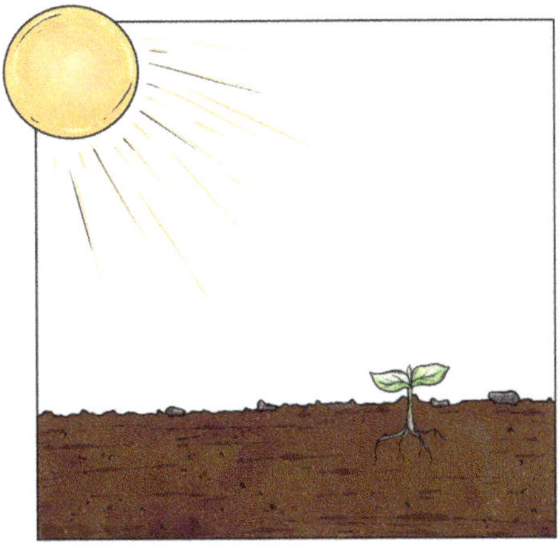

| Day 8

Don't Forget to Smile!

*"A cheerful heart is good medicine,
but a crushed spirit dries up the bones."*

(Prov. 17:22, NIV)

Phyllis Diller once said, "A smile is a curve that sets everything straight,"[4] but what do we do if that smile is hidden? With people masked by masks and social distancing during the pandemic, their faces have been shrouded by a piece of cloth and being at least six feet away. It's so easy to just go about our days with a straight face because no one can really see how you look. Especially in hospitals, where many are gowned and wearing face shields, it may be hard to see how a person really looks physically (externally), let alone how they are feeling emotionally (internally). However, I've heard it said time and again to smile with your eyes, and it's so true. Or even a kind act or simple "How are you, really?" could go a long way. You never know how much of an impact you can make on someone's day—and even life—when you take the time, even a short few minutes, to see how the people around you are really feeling and what they are going through.

As we go about our days through the new norm of things and a post-COVID area, smile every day, even when you can't find a reason to. Be positive. Bring encouragement. Shine bright. Speak light. In a world full of darkness, smile anyway. Jesus in His Word gives us hope that just as we are called to be the light of the world, He is the ultimate light, as mentioned in John 12:46: "I have come as a light to shine in this dark world, so that all who put their trust in me will no longer remain in the dark."

---

[4] "Phyllis Diller Quotes," BrainyQuote, https://1ref.us/mm2.

For some positivity, here are just a few of my favorite quotes for you to enjoy and smile:

~ "Keep smiling … it makes people wonder what you're up to."[5] ~ Sean Keogh
~ "When life gives you a hundred reasons to cry, show life that you have a thousand reasons to smile."[6] ~ Stephenie Meyer
~ "We shall never know all the good that a simple smile can do."[7] ~ Mother Teresa
~ "You are not fully dressed until you wear a smile."[8] ~ Evan Esar
~ "Don't cry because it's over. Smile because it happened."[9] ~ Dr. Seuss

At the end of the day, don't forget to S.M.I.L.E. Spread Much Inspiration Living Every day. ~ Marselinny Mawuntu

It is not always
Easy to self-motivate.
Try it anyway.

Prayer

Dear Lord, I know that You are smiling down on us. We are God's masterpiece and should never take that for granted. We are so loved, so help us to love others as well. In Jesus' name, amen.

Challenge

This challenge may seem like a hard one for some, but walk on your neighborhood street, and introduce yourself to the first new person you meet. Ask them how they're doing and about their day. Continue the conversation and see where it takes you!

---

[5] "Sean Keogh Quotes," Goodreads, https://1ref.us/mm3.
[6] "Stephenie Meyer Quotes," Goodreads, https://1ref.us/mm4.
[7] "Mother Teresa Quotes," BrainyQuote, https://1ref.us/mm5.
[8] "Evan Esar Quotes," AZ Quotes, https://1ref.us/mm6.
[9] "Dr. Seuss Quotes," BrainyQuote, https://1ref.us/mm7.

36 *Living in the Yellow*

| Day 9

Broken into Beautiful

"For we are God's masterpiece. He has created us anew in Christ Jesus, so we can do the good things he planned for us long ago."

(Eph. 2:10, NLT)

A job loss. A family death. A tragic diagnosis. All these things bring unexpected brokenness. What good can really come out of a seemingly shattered situation? In the height of a pandemic, hope seemed hopeless in many places. Believe it or not, it is when we have hit our lowest points—rock bottom—where we really discover the deeper meaning and purpose of life.

If you've never heard of Kintsugi art, it's definitely something to look into! When I first found out about it, I was mind blown. Kintsugi (or kintsukuroi) is a Japanese art that means "to repair with gold." The meaning behind this style of art is to recognize the history of an object (vase, jar, etc.) and to join together what is broken with gold. Instead of hiding its past, this process shows that the product results in something even more beautiful than the original piece. Repairing a broken object whether it's a bowl, plate, or another with golden filling makes the piece unique and stand out; it's a way of showing that the certain piece has a history with value. How much more does this happen to our broken hearts? Although we may not see the gold, Christ refines and restores our brokenness—all our emotional wounds and negative life experiences—and turns it all for our good and His glory. There is much to learn of our Creator.

Years ago, on Father's Day, my family and I went on an adventure. After hours of deciding on a place to go, we ended up going to a place we've never been to before. It was at a waterfront beach down the shore, and to my surprise, there was a mini art show at the entrance, showcasing various mosaic art pieces. One in particular that caught my attention the most was that of a bird, alone, soaring high in the sky above the boats and the waves. It reminded me that often, the waves will hit you out of nowhere, and your options are either: 1) Run behind, or 2) Rise above. It hit me then that broken pieces can result in something truly beautiful, and the thought just resonated with me. Despite the brokenness of your past, or even present, God is working in and with you to make a beautiful work of art: His masterpiece. You may not see it now, but what He has in store is better than anything you could ever imagine. Only He can use what was broken and make it into something beautiful.

Waiting in wonder
Is greater than waiting in
Worry—make your wish.

Prayer

Dear heavenly Father, You were broken to make me whole. Without the sacrifice of Christ, we would not be saved. We praise You for Your amazing grace. In Jesus' name, amen.

Challenge

Find a broken object in your home, and if you have all the missing pieces, put them together with glue and a glittery gold paint (if you have) and put it on display for all to see!

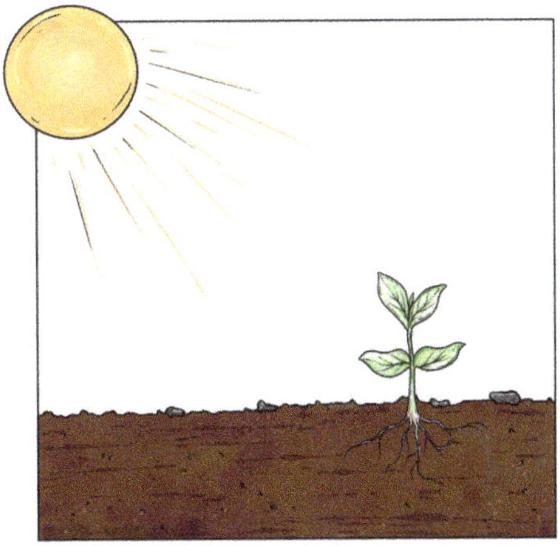

| Day 10

RESTART

"Therefore we also, since we are surrounded by so great a cloud of witnesses, let us lay aside every weight, and the sin which so easily ensnares us, and let us run with endurance the race that is set before us."

(Heb. 12:1, NKJV)

We live in an age of cancel culture, where it's so easy to cancel someone or something without a second thought. There are many miracles that Jesus performed in the Bible, where He could have canceled and shunned these people, but He didn't. The three that stand out to me are the miracles of the deaf/mute man (Mark 7:31–37), the blind man (Mark 8:22–26), and the lame man (John 5:1–9). With the deaf/mute man, sometimes we need to step away from the crowd, away from the noise, to really hear God. When we are at our lowest points and do not have the words to say or don't know where to even begin, Jesus understands. With the blind man, often our vision is blurred due to a lack of faith that He is able to do miracles. Like the lyrics of the song, "While I Wait" by Lincoln Brewster, say: "Sometimes miracles take time."[10] It reminds me that on some occasions according to His will, God can perform a miracle in an instant with immediate recovery. However, other times it may be long. It's a process, and it's a journey, but when we get to the other side, it'll be worthwhile in the end. Lastly, with the lame man, the hardest step is often the first, but once you make that move, you're already on your way.

In retrospect, all of these Bible characters, too, could've said, "Nope, I'm done. I give up. Cancel." With the little energy they had left, they mustered

---

[10] "While I Wait," Genius, https://1ref.us/mm8.

all the faith in their being (as small as a mustard seed), maybe even smaller than a grain of sand, and the Lord took that and blessed it. Likewise, if you keep Him first and focus on things that truly matter (fixing our eyes on heavenly things), miracles can and will still happen. It's all about perspective; it's all in our thinking. How we portray things will eventually become reality.

Practically everything is publicized now. We click on trending, and we see the latest news, mostly negative and depressing stories. We click on social media newsfeed, and we see racial injustice, among other sensitive topics. Although the dread of disease is on the rise, the hope of healing reaches higher than the skies. News Flash: 2020 Wasn't Canceled. Our present situation isn't canceled. With a change of heart, we do the best that we can in every part, and as a sunrise signals the beginning of a new day, instead of clicking cancel, let's all click RESTART.

Start small and work tall.
As a baby learns to walk,
She first learns to crawl.

Prayer

Dear God, You are awesome and wonderful, and over all things, You are sovereign. Let us not give up our days to the negativity and stigma of this world, but as each new day gives us a new start, help us to restart our hearts and rewire our thinking. In Jesus' name, amen.

Challenge

Try the 24-hour "no complaining" challenge. For the next full day, submit to not groan and grumble about your daily routine, and you'll be surprised to see what results flourish from it. Only positivity … no complaints!

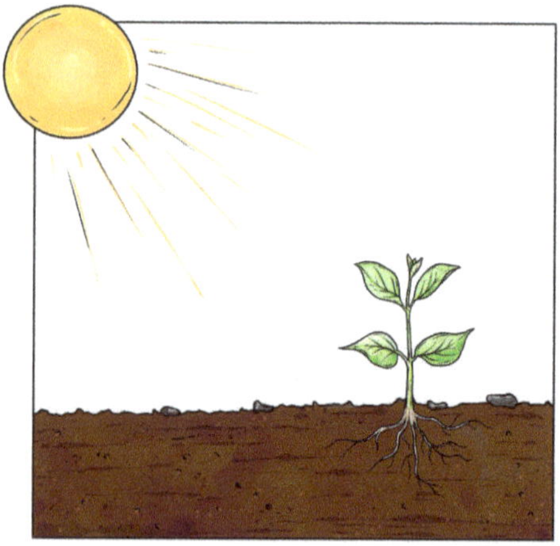

| Day 11

Chosen to Shine

"Let your light so shine before men, that they may see your good works and glorify your Father in heaven."

(Matt. 5:16, NKJV)

What are some things that you are afraid of? What are your deepest fears? It may be the dark, loneliness, unknown, or even all three.... During the times we are currently living in, we are faced with a load of uncertainty, doubt, and fear. Whatever it is we are facing and whatever we are fearing, let's delve into some ways to shift our perspective and gain more of a positive clarity.

A few friends and I had a bonfire recently, and it just reminded me of the good times. When you think of a fire, what three qualities come to mind? Personally, I think of light, warmth, and direction. It's funny because three of my biggest fears as mentioned before (the dark, loneliness, and the unknown) in a way have an opposite correlation to what a fire can bring about. To overcome my fear of the dark, I actually took a caving class in university, which was way out of my comfort zone! Sometimes it's hard for us to see the light at the end of the tunnel, or cave, but Jesus calls us to be a light to a world of death, destruction, and darkness. Moreover, a fire also can symbolize warmth, and with loneliness, you often feel cold and isolated from others around you. Especially with being socially distant at times, it may be easy for us to feel like no one is really wanting to interact and connect. It's true that others give us warmth through physical hugs, words of affirmation, etc. We should not fear isolation when the Lord is always near. Lastly, when you are lost in the unknown, you long for and pray for a sense of direction and God's leading in your life. Walking in faith requires taking a step that you can't even see is there. He is our ultimate

GPS (God's Positioning System), where He guides and provides when you abide and not hide. Even though we don't know what the future holds, we can rest assured because we know who holds the future. When life changes, God stays the same.

So, why is this topic important for us right now? God uses our fears to remind us that we are "chosen to shine" above them all. In 1 Peter 2:9 (NKJV), it is written, "But you are a chosen generation, a royal priesthood, a holy nation, His own special people, that you may proclaim the praises of Him who called you out of darkness into His marvelous light." With F.E.A.R., you have two options: You can "Forget Everything and Run" or "Face Everything and Rise."

The choice is yours.

*Lasting change comes from
Microscopic habits that
Build a foundation.*

Prayer

Dear Jehovah Jireh, You are our provider. We have nothing to fear. I pray that you will let our faith be greater than our fear. Help us to remember that You are near. In Jesus' name, amen.

Challenge

Write down your greatest fear(s) and read these verses over them:
- 2 Timothy 1:7
- 1 John 4:18
- Psalm 56:4

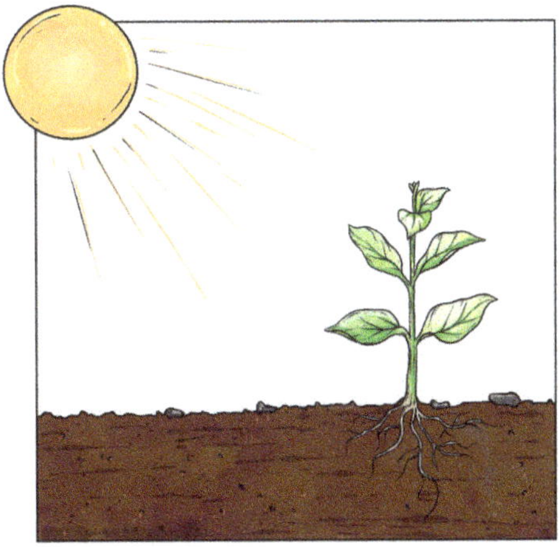

Day 12

A Winning Attitude

"But sanctify the Lord God in your hearts, and always be ready to give a defense to everyone who asks you a reason for the hope that is in you, with meekness and fear."

(1 Peter 3:15, NKJV)

I love the fall season, though winter is my favorite. However, there's just something about fall with all its beautiful colors, shades, and cool weather that initiates the start of flannel shirts and warm cocoa. We have come so far throughout this journey, and it amazes me how God has led and will continue to lead us for the years to come. God is good even when our situation is not. Although this world is constantly changing, He remains the same. He is the only constant in our lives, and He is the same yesterday, today, and forever. With the ups and downs of our current situation, it may be easier to steer into the direction of negativity and doubt, but with a winning attitude in our lives, we can bring joy and hope to others.

How can we develop a winning attitude when preaching the gospel or even just in life? Sometimes, it is so difficult to stay positive in an environment that seems so dreary and hopeless. There have been times when the negative overwhelms and feels overpowering of my life, but here's an acronym that I gleaned from Sabbath lessons as well as my own personal experiences. It's called S.E.A.T.

1. Speak Words of Life
   - John 4:27–30, 39–42
2. Emphasize Positivity
   - Matthew 15:21–28, Mark 14:6–9

3. Accept Others' Differences
   - Romans 15:7, Ephesians 4:32
4. Teach Truth in Love
   - 2 Timothy 4:2, Titus 3:4–5

When we take a S.E.A.T. at Jesus' feet, we can develop a winning attitude toward everyone we meet. When we live to encourage and uplift others, especially during most difficult times, we in turn are richly blessed. No matter our situation, if we shift our perspective from negative to positive, humbly giving God all of our control, we can win at any season of life, even the winter storms!

In order to live
The life that you want to live:
You need to just breathe.

Prayer

Dear Mighty Savior, seasons change but You never do. Your love for us is constant and courageous. Thank You, Lord, for being our source of comfort and hope, and may we strive to lead others closer to You each and every day. In Jesus' name, amen.

Challenge

Whatever season you are in right now (in life or winter/spring/summer/fall), reminisce about the good parts about what you enjoy and share them with someone you love. Spread His goodness!

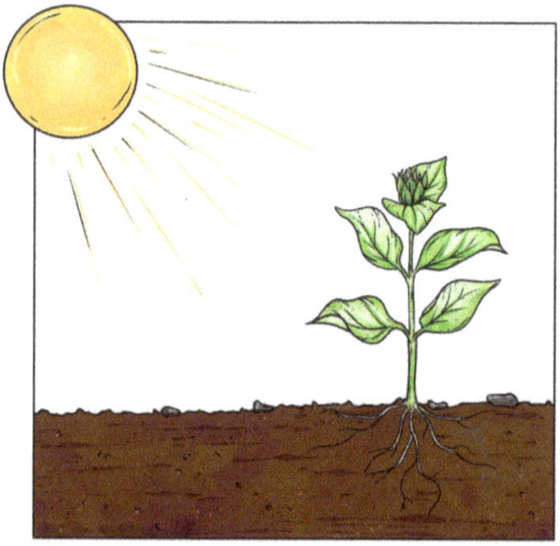

| Day 13

Blessings in Disguise

"To everything there is a season, a time for every purpose under heaven."

(Eccles. 3:1, NKJV)

Have you ever experienced a sudden change? If you have lived life long enough, you definitely would have. From leaves changing into beautiful bright colors to the weather getting a lot cooler than before, seasons are true indicators that change is in process, one way or another.

When we are waiting for something to change, we often miss all the things that are happening in us to change us for the better. Walking through spiritual valleys may seem never-ending, but you're not alone. If you've read the Old Testament, you've probably come across the phrase, "It came to pass." It appears over and over again, whether it's mentioning the floodwaters covering the earth or God giving the Promised Land to the Israelites. Notice the phrase is not "It came to stay." The same goes for your spiritual low. It will not be like this forever. It too will pass.

A short story I'd like to share started in a place I didn't think I would fit in. A new job environment that didn't necessarily "fit" my interests or expectations, but I felt God calling me to stay until this season passed, but it came with a lot of doubt in the journey and asking God why He put me there in the first place. I felt so lost and confused; I didn't know what to do. Sometimes we look for a yes or no to our questions, when God's third option is simply not yet.

During this time, I met a sweet older woman at a doctor's office, and she asked me to wait with her and if I could bring her back home since she had no one else to take her. Miles and miles away from her residence, I agreed and with a smile on her face, she thanked me and asked if there was anything she could do or give me a later time, as she had nothing with her now. I kindly declined the offer, but she insisted on getting at least something—an email/home address, anything. I didn't think much of it, and to make her feel better, I actually just scribbled something illegible on pen and paper in hopes she wouldn't be able to read it. I dropped her off in the late hours of the night, we exchanged prayers, and I never saw her again.

Fast-forward seven months later, I was at an all-time low with the stress of this job, and I wanted to quit working. Until one day, right when I needed it, a small box came to my home. *That's strange,* I thought to myself, *I didn't order anything in the mail recently.* To my surprise, there was a handwritten note card with cute little antiques bundled in bubble wrap from the same lady as she described our previous interaction. In His perfect timing, this blessing in disguise was exactly what I needed at that time to help me push through, and when all seemed dark, be a light.

Birds sing, blossoms bloom
Bears sleep, branches break (but soon)
Beautiful sunshine.

Prayer

Dear heavenly Father, sometimes we don't know why things happen the way they do, but You always work all things out for good. Thank You, Lord, for being good. In Jesus' name, amen.

Challenge

Write a handwritten card of appreciation to someone special and mail it to them without notice.

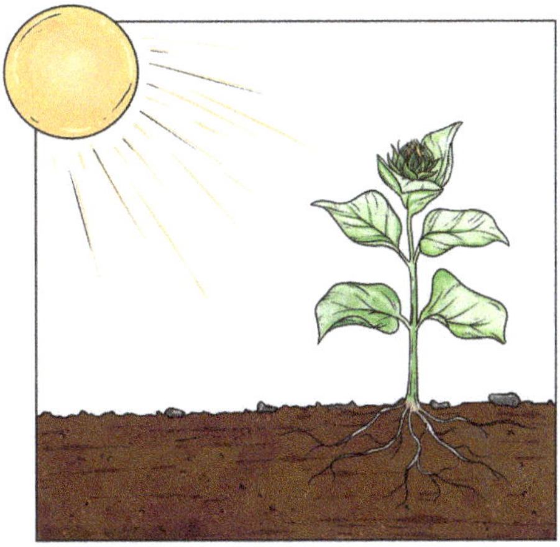

Day 14

Finding Joy in the Desert

"Now an angel of the Lord spoke to Philip, saying, 'Arise and go toward the south along the road which goes down from Jerusalem to Gaza.' This is desert."

(Acts 8:26, NKJV)

Dry. Distant. Desolate. These are some adjectives that could be used to describe a desert. Not a very ideal place, is it? A lot of times, we find ourselves in times of desert where nothing seems to be going right or things seem out of place. We try to keep walking forward only to be scorched by unexpected trials and tribulations. The sandy dunes leave us confused as to which direction we need to go to get to our destination. We are thirsting for water that never runs dry, but I have good news. There is joy to be found.

If we look at the first five words of the next verse of our key text, in Acts 8:27 (NKJV), it says: "So he arose and went." That was it. No question; no doubt. Philip got up and obeyed the command. Despite not knowing where he was going or how he would get there, he still went. And it was in the desert where he found the joy of bringing someone to Christ—the Ethiopian eunuch. Someone unexpected that God expected for him to meet along the way for this divine appointment. If we submit to the Lord our plans and desires, if we remember who is in control, if we venture out of our comfort zone to where He calls us to go, we will truly experience the joy of the Lord through service through Him and for Him. Whether or not we feel "good enough" to go where He is taking us in life, let us not put any limit to our limitless God. He is more than enough and always enough.

He is more than enough and always enough—so we are enough.

I remember a time when my family and I were walking down a concrete street in the middle of nowhere, bathed with trash bags, flies, and half-emptied bottles. There were many cracks along the road, which made me wonder about all that had happened throughout the history of this foreign territory. Then I saw it. A lone, small flower flourishing through the cracks in all its beauty. One of my favorite quotes I have hanging on my room wall says, "Bloom where you are planted." And there is so much truth to it. It doesn't matter where you are. Be there fully and completely without complaint. We can truly find joy in the desert … we just have to look for it.

There's always something
To be thankful for in life
You just have to look.

Prayer

Dear Lord, thank You for being the Water of Life in a dry, thirsty land. Only You have the power to quench our unmet desires and expectations. Help us to look to You in all things, and let us truly be where You have called us to be. In Jesus' name, amen.

Challenge

Take a moment to stop and smell the roses (if you don't live near a place with roses, any flower works too!). Spend time in gratitude remembering that the Creator of the universe clothed you and blessed you even more than you could ever imagine.

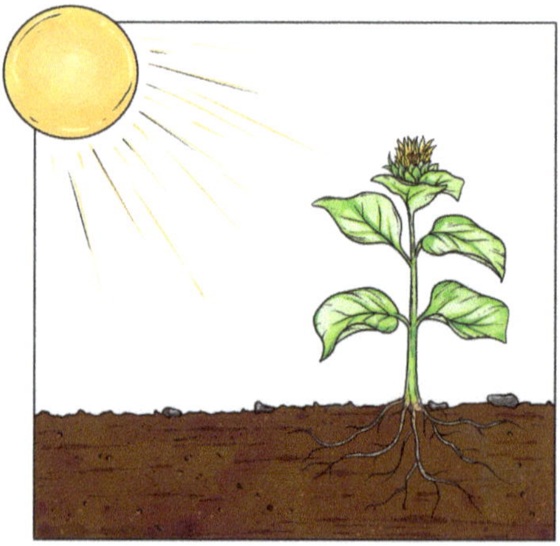

> Day 15

No One Is an Island

"A friend loves at all times, and a brother is born for a time of adversity."

(Prov. 17:17, NIV)

If you were stranded on an island, what is the one thing you would bring with you? While you're taking the time to think of an answer, I wanted to mention that in the past, I, along with some family and church friends, were actually stranded on an island—but for camping purposes! It was a fun, enjoyable time. We had an island home for a weekend, and it was amazing to experience and connect with God through nature, away from any stresses or responsibilities. Though there was very limited phone connection, it was a safe haven.

Now, I'm sure everyone is all too familiar with a "new norm" post COVID-19 pandemic. Wearing masks, being six feet apart, and social distancing separates us from one another, in a way like being isolated on an island, distant socially from others and the rest of the world around you. Overall, it may seem lonely, fearful, or depressing, as we humans were very much created for a sense of community, loving others as Christ Himself loves us. We wore these physical (surgical or nonsurgical) masks to protect us from a virus, yet often, we don't realize that we wear an emotional mask to cover up how we truly feel. We don't want others to see what's going on inside. This invisible mask that others can't see. But God sees. God sees who you truly are, from the mask you wear pretending that everything is okay to the mask that doesn't let people in for fear of letting your guard down and getting hurt later. Sometimes, we build our own walls of defense that isolate us from those around us, and we push away those who are trying to help. Ever been in that situation?

I want to leave you with three key encouraging points, or the three *C*'s, that can help us focus on our mental/emotional health and actually care about the interests of others as well as our own:

1) Call, 2) Check, and 3) Change. Call on others and, more importantly, call on God when times get tough. Check up on those who you haven't seen or heard from in a while, as God never fails to check on us. Lastly, in this manner, you could even change a life; God does the same and changes our lives for the better when we live for Him alone. Remember: No one is an island. God is always there for us. May we do the same also and be there for one another like family.

Communication
And preparation are keys
That unlock success.

Prayer

Dear Father God, keep us in constant communication with You. From the start of our day to the very end, let our lives be a never-ending prayer of thanksgiving and praise to Your holy name. Help us to reach out to others as You always do for us. In Jesus' name, amen.

Challenge

Try the three *C*'s. Have one person in mind (or even two or three!) to call up, check on, and change his or her day, according to God's will and grace.

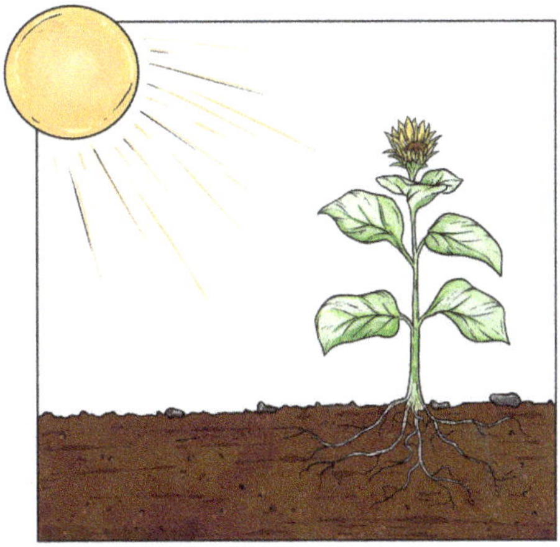

| **Day 16**

Stuck in the Muck

"I waited patiently for the LORD; he turned to me and heard my cry. He lifted me out of the slimy pit, out of the mud and mire; he set my feet on a rock and gave me a firm place to stand."

(Ps. 40:1–2, NIV)

The day started off as a regular Sabbath morning. It was a beautiful (surprisingly warm) fall day, spending time with family. I had no prior meetings or engagements that day, so my afternoon was virtually free—a peaceful, relaxing way to end the week. Then spontaneously, some of my family members decided to go on a faraway adventure, so I made up my mind to tag along. Little did I know what lay ahead....

This is some rocky terrain, I had thought to myself as we drove on to our surprise destination. It was too late to turn back now, so I took some photo and video footage just in case we got lost. Soon after, I lost signal and connection was cut off for most of us as we sat in the Toyota 4Runner, surrounded by the wilderness. By the grace of God, we later found our friends we were meeting up with and drove around through the thick woods, when all of a sudden—*THUD!* We were stuck. Not the "easily get out by maneuvering around" stuck. I mean, stuck stuck. Minutes trickled into hours as we tried every attempt to push the car from the muddy pit back on the firm ground. But we didn't give up. We couldn't just abandon the car in the middle of nowhere. By this time, sunset hit and the darkness seemed inevitable in these woods. Afraid of what lurked in the distance, I stayed and prayed inside the warmth of the car. Miraculously, after this arduous ordeal ended, we managed to have the car towed back to safety.

How many times in life do you find yourselves "stuck in the muck" of whatever situation you are in? Do you feel like sometimes it's so hard to get out, even almost impossible? Pushing one step forward only to move three steps back? And you're waiting for an answer, for help from anyone who can get you out of the mess. That's physically how we felt that night; no matter how much we tried, the car did not budge an inch. How about spiritually? As it says in the key verse, hold on to the Lord and wait for Him. He is able and willing to deliver you from any slimy pit, bringing you back to a solid place. Our God is in the business of towing burdened hearts from the brokenness in the world. He's only a call away with a connection better than any 5G out there. And the best part is? He doesn't even charge.

When in doubt, look up.
How can you see the night stars
When you're looking down?

Prayer

Dear God, we praise You for sending Your Son, Jesus, to come down to earth and rescue us from our slimy, sticky sin. You make unstuck what is stuck from what we or others have done. Thank You for being our Savior. In Jesus' name, amen.

Challenge

Next time you see someone stuck on the road or who seems to be in need, prayerfully ask God for a willing heart and offer to help in a way that you can. Bring a friend for support if you need!

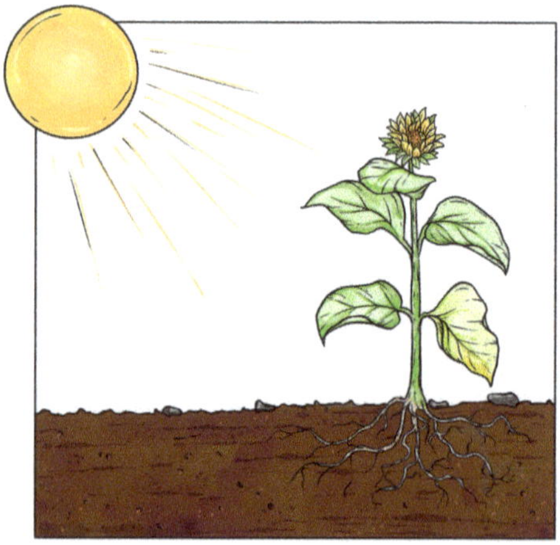

Day 17

Thank You, COVID-19

"Then he said to them, 'Go your way, eat the fat, drink the sweet, and send portions to those for whom nothing is prepared; for this day is holy to our Lord. Do not sorrow, for the joy of the LORD is your strength.'"

(Neh. 8:10, NKJV)

Wow, 2020 was such a year! Through everything that has happened, it's crazy to look back at where we were in the beginning and see how far we've come. I'm amazed to see the amount of growth that took place and blessings that came about in the most unexpected places. During the Thanksgiving holidays, my desire is for us all to truly have an attitude of gratitude and not forget the Reason for the season—and every season in our lives. I think it is so easy for us to complain or grumble (myself included!) that we lose sight of what's important. Although times have been hard for a lot of us, I encourage you to look harder for that silver lining that is still there and to take time right now, just a few minutes, to write down what you are thankful for (three things or more). Below is an outline example but be specific with your gratitude; include why.

1. Devotional time with God because it helps me have a great start and end to my days
2. Family bonding on weekends because we get to catch up on updates with one another
3. Golden friendships because they have lasted the test of time and remain true to this day

As the key Bible verse above says, which suits our Thanksgiving theme, may we not be sad about the bad things that came about these past few months. With the countless blessings we have, and God continues to give, let us give back to Him by serving others who don't have, feeding the homeless, reaching out to those in need, and focusing on praise. Amidst the increasing numbers of crime, illness, war, famine, and more, I pray that our faith may increase all the more. With that, as strange as it may sound, thank you, COVID-19, for without you, I would not be writing this. And thank you to all … (insert difficult and trying moments or events here). You are a blessing in disguise.

How can you not see?
That everything around you
Was meant to be free.

Prayer

Dear heavenly Father, we are forever grateful for Your love and compassion. Thank You that in Christ, we can have freedom and peace that surpasses all understanding. In Jesus' name, amen.

Challenge

As mentioned, write down your gratitude. What are you thankful for today? Why are you thankful? Praise God for His goodness and reflect on His mercy.

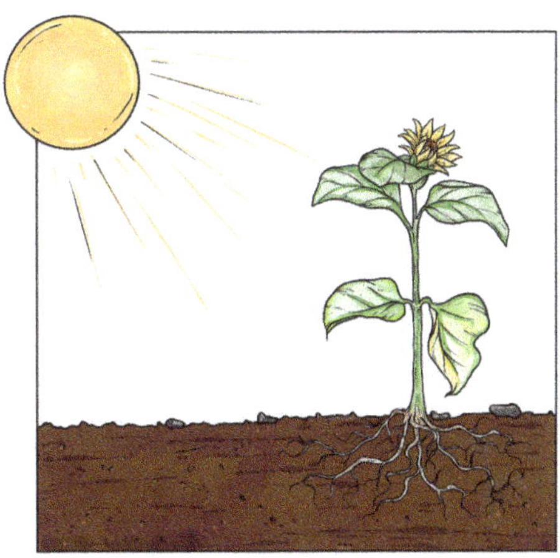

| **Day 18**

Beginning or Ending

"Neither do people pour new wine into old wineskins. If they do, the skins will burst; the wine will run out and the wineskins will be ruined. No, they pour new wine into new wineskins, and both are preserved."

(Matt. 9:17, NIV)

As we begin new days, months, and years, we end certain chapters and specific seasons. For me, endings are usually bittersweet (more bitter than sweet), but maybe most of us can agree that a hard year, like 2020 in particular, would be a sweeter end. The start of a new year, 2021, seemed promising, but a key takeaway that I want to leave you with today is that pressing on to the future means letting go of things that are holding you back in the past. Let me explain. . . .

The Bible mentions in chapter 9 of Matthew about the concept of pouring new wine into old wineskins. Now, in context, Jesus here is talking about fasting when He was questioned on it. When talking about "new wine," I believe He's talking about a new life—a new way of thinking. If your perspective is changed for the better, why would you go back to your old way of living? In the same way, as we approach a new era, let us not take the negativity, the doubt, and the fear into the new. When an old chapter closes, through faith in Jesus, we know the best is yet to come.

When summer ended, and fall began, a group of friends and I went to a new nature area to go hiking and exploring. We had a great time for our afternoon Sabbath program with praise and worship, personal prayer time, games, and a powerful message that we all needed. At the end of the day, I recall feeling a bit sad that the day was ending, and thoughts of insecurity and nostalgia crept into my mind. I remember asking my friends that evening after we had gone out, "Do you all prefer sunrises or sunsets?"

Side note: we actually ended the day by taking a group picture in front of the sunset! I received some profound, thoughtful answers about the beauty of landscapes, what they signify, and so on, but I want to ask you the same question today. Which one? Whether sunrises (beginnings) or sunsets (endings), one thing to keep in mind that I learned throughout life is that, whichever you choose, what's more are the memories made in the middle.

So many times, so
Many faces and places
You can be the change.

Prayer

Dear Lord, God we cherish the beauty of Your creation, the nature landscapes, the unique wildlife, and everything in between. You are the Alpha and Omega, the Beginning and the End. Let us trust fully and completely in Your time and give up all control. In Jesus' name, amen.

Challenge

See for yourself if you are able to wake up bright and early, before the break of dawn, and go to the nearest nature spot to watch the sun rise. In the same way and day, watch the sun set and reflect on your thoughts throughout the day—the ups and downs and everything in the middle.

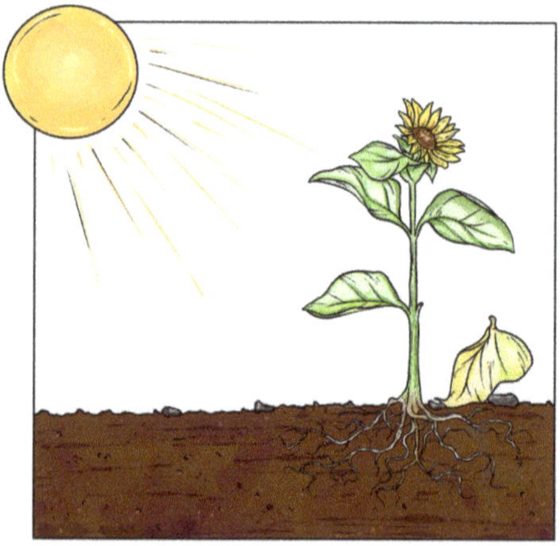

| Day 19

Qualifying the Called

"Then the LORD asked him, 'What is that in your hand?'
'A shepherd's staff,' Moses replied. 'Throw it down on the ground,'
the LORD told him. So Moses threw down the staff, and it turned
into a snake! Moses jumped back."

(Exod. 4:2–3, NLT)

Have you ever felt like you were the most unqualified person for a job, a position, a role? I'm sure that's exactly how many of the Bible heroes felt, like Gideon and David, just to name a few. The weakest, the smallest, the least of these, but that is exactly where God's strength, might, and abundance come in. His strength is made perfect in our weakness, but sometimes we forget. God does not see us how we see ourselves but who we could become if we just let Him lead us. As Mark Batterson once said, "God doesn't call the qualified; He qualifies the called."[11]

I want to focus today on the story and call of Moses. Based on the Bible key text, we find Moses in a dialogue with the Lord, who asks a simple yet straightforward question: "What is that in your hand?" To me, it's like God is asking, "What do you have that I have given you?" Then Moses responds, "A shepherd's staff." I can picture him shrugging his shoulders and wondering what he is supposed to do with a sorry rod. A plain old stick, but with the little, the simple, the humble things we have in our lives, like the loaves of bread and fish, if we give them all to God, He can multiply it. Instead of making excuses, I want to start making examples. Instead of fearing the future, I want to praise God in the present. And instead of hiding behind

---

[11] "Mark Batterson Quotes," QuoteFancy, https://1ref.us/mm9.

a mask of insecurity and doubt, I want to be hidden behind the shadow of the cross. Changing your internal monologue and negative thinking to one that is positive can truly change your whole life.

You may be thinking, *I'm not good enough* or you're waiting to get out of the rut that you're in. Jesus is more than able and willing to qualify those He has made for a special purpose. Every day is a new day and a new opportunity to make things count for the kingdom of heaven. We are all called to do something for the Lord. Whatever it is, He will make it so clear to you, in His timing, what your calling on this earth is and why He created you. As quoted by Mark Twain: "The two most important days in your life are the day you are born and the day you find out why."[12] So, what does it mean to be called? No matter what trials are met, we have a mission. No matter where we are placed, we have a purpose. No matter why the doors are closed, we have a calling. We are called, chosen, and cherished by Him. He is calling you, me, all of us today.... The question is, will we answer?

Love God. Love yourself.
Love others. The golden rule.
The greatest command.

Prayer

Dear God, Lord we are called by You, chosen for a season, and cherished by Your love. When at times we think we are not fit for the job, use us anyway. For Your glory. In Jesus' name, amen.

Challenge

Try this activity next time you are by the beach. Grab some rocks and be by the sand. The rocks symbolize your priorities in life and the sand comes secondary to fill up your time. Using a big glass jar or clear bucket, put the rocks inside first and let the sand fill in the gaps (try it the opposite way with sand first then rocks and see the difference it makes—you run out of room!).

---

[12] "Mark Twain Quotes," Goodreads, https://1ref.us/mm10.

| **Day 20**

Worry Is a Waste

"Can any one of you by worrying add a single hour to your life?"

(Matt. 6:27, NIV)

How many of you are worried about something right now? How many of you feel like even this week has been a lot for you or you just have a lot on your mind? Whether it's finances, family, friends, or even the food that you're planning on eating later, often we find ourselves burdened with a load of cares. We wonder, does Jesus care? Like a favorite hymn of mine "Does Jesus Care?" says: "O yes, He cares, I know He cares. His heart is touched with my grief; When the days are weary, The long night dreary, I know my Savior cares."[13] When our minds are clouded with thoughts of anxiety or fear about the future and what it holds, how good is it to just praise Him through singing, knowing that He will take us through, amen?

It's easier said than done though, I know. Let's turn to the Word for some encouragement and enlightenment in Matthew 6:25–34 (the sermon on the mount). Now, before we read this passage on not worrying, isn't it interesting to note that, like in this passage's setting, there are many scenes in the Bible referring to mountains or hills? The sermon on the mount, Mount Sinai, and Calvary's hill. High places, but what about the low places? The valleys or the plains. When I think of a time of prayer and fasting in the Bible, I think about when Jesus was at the foot of the Mount of Olives at the Garden of Gethsemane, pleading to the Father that His will be done. That was a very low point—more weight and burden than we could ever imagine carrying. Yet these verses remind us that worrying is a waste of time;

---

[13] "Does Jesus care when my heart is pained," Hymnal.net, https://1ref.us/mm11.

it doesn't add to our life, it only takes away from it. Worry means we don't trust the God of the universe. But He will always take care of us.

Through the hills and valleys, mountains and plains, finding time to pray and reflect on the goodness of God and to praise Him in the storms of death, brokenness, suffering, is where we find true healing. That is where we find true joy. That is where we find true strength. Jesus tells us we don't need to worry about tomorrow. He's already there! The God of our past, present, and future knows the end from the beginning, and it's a good story. Maybe people, too, have asked you, "So what are your plans after X, Y, and Z?" You name it. When we can't see what's ahead, it takes real faith to give all control to Him, to let go and let God. With this, I want to assure you: Why worry about anything when Jesus is our everything?

The future seems far
Feels like it will never come …
'Til you blink your eyes.

Prayer

Dear Mighty Savior, forgive us when we worry and doubt Your power and goodness in our lives. Everything is safe with You. Thank You for the Holy Spirit who is our comforter in hard times. In Jesus' name, amen.

Challenge

Write down all your worries and cares that you have on your mind right now on a piece of paper. Physically crumple the paper into a ball and take joy in throwing it out in the trash, knowing that those thoughts have no dominion over you when you give up control to the Lord of all.

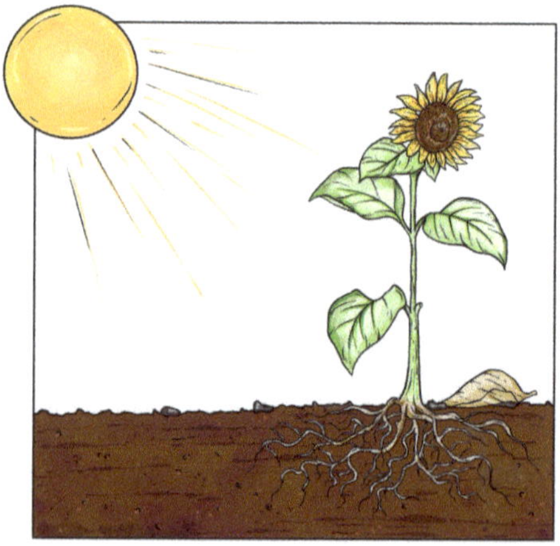

| Day 21

What Are You Waiting For?

"'For I know the plans I have for you,' declares the LORD, 'plans to prosper you and not to harm you, plans to give you hope and a future.'"

(Jer. 29:11, NIV)

I was six feet under for about six seconds before I realized what was happening. Seconds seemed like eternity to me, and there were only two options. *Sink or swim*, I thought to myself, but I was stuck in the middle. I did not want to sink, but I also did not know how to swim. Like a traffic light, there is red, yellow, or green; I was in the yellow. I was only about ten, and I felt anxious and helpless. When my heroic sister realized the dilemma and swam over to my splashing, squalling scene, I took hold of her arm, rose up, and found purpose in that waiting. Although living in the yellow is a time of uncertainty, it is during this exact moment that we find our true human purpose to be compassionate, patient, and resilient as we serve and save others.

Throughout my life experiences, initially I felt a sense of inadequacy in being able to help those who could not help themselves, as I also faced a similar time with that incident. However, it was during my time as a volunteer outreach leader for a camp where I met (we'll call him) T. In spending time with local community kids in the area, we were exposed to how underserved and poor some families were. Yet T remained ingrained in my mind due to his vibrant energy and desire to learn. "Monkey bars!" he exclaimed, as he grabbed my arm running to the playground. This charming little boy climbed up the ladder but looked up in fear. "Don't worry, I'll hold you. Give it a try," I said as he mirrored my smile. After he finally made it to the other side, he never once stopped smiling to have a good time. Even in his current crisis circumstance, he chose joy.

Similarly, through mission trips abroad, I gained a deeper sense of service even in my seasons of waiting. One encounter I had with a patient in a free health clinic visit changed my view of what it means to truly serve. Most of the patients had diabetes and this one in particular had a gangrene foot and was reluctant to have me treat and bandage her wound because it would take a long time. Despite not knowing how long the process would be, I assured her that, as long as it takes, I will strive to do my utmost best to care for her condition, regardless of time. That interaction allowed her to let me help when she could not help herself, and it was a spiritually healing moment for the both of us. Truly, it is such a powerful thing to be heard and understood.

Ultimately, I am glad that I did not need CPR when I almost drowned that time, but now, I have a greater understanding of what it means to have Compassion, Patience, and Resilience in times of waiting and being there for others in their times as well. Living in the yellow does not mean that life is over; it means that it is possible to find joy to rise above the unprecedented times of uncertain unknowns. Now, many years later, praise God, I am a much better swimmer.

Know that everything
Is going to be okay.
Faith greater than fear.

Prayer

Dear heavenly Father, thank You for being with us in the waiting, and while we await Your soon coming, let us be ready. Prepare our hearts and minds in spirit and truth. In Jesus' name, amen.

Challenge

Take time to be still and know that He is God. Spend time in prayer; take as long as you need.

Day 21 75

Afterword

We are all waiting
Room to grow and room to show
That we are ready.

As the sun sets, another day ends. There is no space for regret for the things we'll forget in time. Everything that happened had a reason, whether we believe it or not. Even the darkest moments of night remind us that a new dawn will break, and there is joy in the morning. In the stillness and silence of the void black skies, when we look up in the faint distance, the stars shine the brightest. Earth anticipates the tomorrow sun but can wait, with no rush, as the small speck emerges into radiant light. And the seed planted will sleep in peace knowing a new day brings new life and growth, even though the process is slow.... Flowers don't worry, so why should we?

Congratulations on making it to Day 21! You did it. However, I have some news for you. This is not the end. It's only the beginning of your continued devotional life journey. I pray that as we are all living in the yellow, we live it out to the fullest, despite any setbacks that come our way. Living yellow means living joyfully—*a vibrant life that radiates love and light to everyone we meet*. We must live our waiting seasons in confidence and faith, knowing that everything will be okay in the end. If you realize that it's not okay, then keep going; it's not the end. It gets better.

One last story I'll share that I've heard a few times before (with different versions) changed my perspective on how to live yellow. This anecdotal story also happens to be in the hospital setting with two patients. We will call the first patient Bob and the second patient Bill. Now, Bob and Bill have been hospital roommates for a long time and have become good friends. Bob had the privilege of having the window side bed, while Bill's bed was by the door. One day, the two were talking, and Bob was describing all the beautiful things he saw outside the window on this sunny day. He illustrated to Bill that the little kids were playing on the playground park, the young couples were eating together on a nice bench, and the kind elderly were feeding the chirping birds. What a magnificent sight he saw, together with bright blue skies, dark green trees.

Days became weeks, and one day, when Bill happened to be asleep, the nurses took Bob out of the room for an urgent medical procedure. Bob never came back. Bill, emotional and in tears, questioned why, and the medical team could give no answer. One strange request Bill asked of them was to move his bed to the window, so at least he could see the beauty that Bob once saw. That window was blocked by a cinder block wall, and Bill later found out that Bob was blind. Don't just live to survive.... Thrive. Inspire others along the way. Maybe, just maybe ...

"The best is yet to come."

The waiting season
Oh, living in the yellow!
A glorious place.

We invite you to view the complete
selection of titles we publish at:
www.TEACHServices.com

We encourage you to write us
with your thoughts about this,
or any other book we publish at:
info@TEACHServices.com

TEACH Services' titles may be purchased in
bulk quantities for educational, fund-raising,
business, or promotional use.
bulksales@TEACHServices.com

Finally, if you are interested in seeing
your own book in print, please contact us at:
publishing@TEACHServices.com

We are happy to review your manuscript at no charge.

www.ingramcontent.com/pod-product-compliance
Lightning Source LLC
Chambersburg PA
CBHW042133160426
43199CB00021B/2898